Weird America!

AMERICA'S ODDEST
LEGENDS

Peachtree

By Caitie McAneney

Gareth Stevens
PUBLISHING

Please visit our website, www.garethstevens.com. For a free color catalog of all our high-quality books, call toll free 1-800-542-2595 or fax 1-877-542-2596.

Cataloging-in-Publication Data

Names: McAneney, Caitie.
Title: America's oddest legends / Caitie McAneney.
Description: New York : Gareth Stevens Publishing, 2016. | Series: Weird America | Includes index.
Identifiers: ISBN 9781482440317 (pbk.) | ISBN 9781482440324 (6 pack) | ISBN 9781482440331 (library bound)
Subjects: LCSH: Legends–United States–Juvenile literature. | United States–Folklore–Juvenile literature. | Tales–United States–Juvenile literature.
Classification: LCC GR105.M384 2016 | DDC 398.20973–dc23

First Edition

Published in 2016 by
Gareth Stevens Publishing
111 East 14th Street, Suite 349
New York, NY 10003

Designer: Sarah Liddell
Editor: Ryan Nagelhout

Photo credits: Cover, p. 1 (arrow) Mascha Tace/Shutterstock.com; cover, p. 1 ullstein bild/Contributor/ullstein bild/ Getty Images; sidebar used throughout zayats-and-zayats/Shutterstock.com; background texture used throughout multipear/Shutterstock.com; p. 5 Lukas Holub/Shutterstock.com; p. 6 © David Barkasy and Loren Coleman; p. 7 (map) Map Resources/Shutterstock.com; p. 7 illustrations by Mickey Harmon; p. 9 Al3xil/Wikimedia Commons; p. 11 FPG/Staff/Archive Photo/Getty Images; p. 13 Hulton Archive/Stringer/Getty Images; p. 15 DcoetzeeBot/Wikimedia Commons; p. 16 Andreas Meyer/Shutterstock.com; p. 17 breakermaximus/Shutterstock.com; p. 19 Photo Image/ Shutterstock.com; p. 20 Tom Grundy/Shutterstock.com; p. 21 Maroonbeard/Wikimedia Commons; p. 22 Ken Thomas/ Wikimedia Commons; p. 23 Jeff martinez/Shutterstock.com; p. 25 David Muir/Getty Images; p. 26 Bob Orsillo/ Shutterstock.com; p. 27 Alexlky/Shutterstock.com; p. 29 Fer Gregory/Shutterstock.com.

Printed in the United States of America

CPSIA compliance information: Batch #CW16GS: For further information contact Gareth Stevens, New York, New York at 1-800-542-2595.

CONTENTS

Words in the glossary appear in **bold** type the first time they are used in the text.

GREAT AMERICAN LEGENDS

America is a land of many stories. Some are legends, which are stories passed down through time that can't be proven true. Settlers from other parts of the world brought legends and **traditions** from their home countries. Still other legends grew from events that took place in America, from settling the western **frontier** to the rise of railroads.

Some legends are based around a central character, a hero. Some are tall tales, or unbelievable stories filled with **cryptids** and monsters. Some are scary, while others are funny. And some are just plain odd!

Living Heritage

Some odd legends and traditions made it to America when settlers arrived. They told legends to keep their **heritage** alive. For example, Germans who moved to Pennsylvania brought the legend of Belsnickel, one of St. Nicholas's—or Santa Claus's—friends. The strange, dirt-covered man roamed the countryside dressed all in furs and could tell if children had been good or bad that year!

Legends connect us to history and give Americans a common story. They add to American **culture**. And some are just fun to tell!

5

MONSTERS AND CRYPTIDS

America is filled with stories about cryptids and monsters. Take, for example, the Loveland Frog. In 1955, an Ohio businessman spotted a creature with green skin and weblike hands under a bridge. The creature was spotted again in 1972 when police saw a man with a froglike face jump off a bridge!

Another monster, the skunk ape, was spotted in Florida starting in the 1960s. The ape gets its name from its smell, which is like rotting eggs or **methane**. In 2000, a woman claimed to take a photo of the skunk ape in her backyard. She said the creature crept into her backyard and stole apples from her porch three nights in a row!

skunk ape

"Tessie"

Did you know that Lake Tahoe has its own version of the Loch Ness Monster? Called "Tessie," the beast was first spotted in an underground tunnel beneath Cave Rock by native settlers in the 19th century. Some think that Tessie is actually a dinosaur. They think it's a plesiosaur, ichthyosaur, or mosasaur.

CRYPTIDS OF NORTH AMERICA

Lliamna Lake Monster

Waheela

Adlet

Shuswaggi

Ogoogo

Turtle Lake Monster

Manipogo

Wendigo

Sasquatch

Shunka Warakin

Beast of Bray Road

Frogman

Memphre

Dover Demon

Sharlie

Champ

Tessie

Bear Lake Monster

Thunderbird

Pope Lick Monster

Mothman

Jersey Devil

Mongollon Monster

Skinwalker

Oklahoma Octopus

Ozark Howler

Scope Ore Swamp Lizard Man

Lake Worth Monster

Altamaha-ha

Swamp Ape

Chupacabra

THE JERSEY DEVIL

One of the oldest legends in American history is that of the Jersey Devil. One telling is that the Leeds family settled near the Pine Barrens in New Jersey. Their 13th child, however, escaped the house and became a devil!

The creature—also called the Leeds Devil—is said to look like a kangaroo, walking on two legs with **cloven hooves**. It also has wings like a bat and a horselike head. Some sightings say the Jersey Devil has a tail like a reptile. The monster is said to be responsible for the deaths of dogs, chickens, and other small animals, and leaves odd footprints in its wake.

Cold Devil

In 1982, the Colorado Rockies hockey team of the National Hockey League moved to New Jersey. After a statewide search for a new team name, the franchise decided to name the team after the Jersey Devil. Some people didn't like the name because they thought they were talking about the figure in religious stories.

This image of the Jersey Devil is from a 1909 Philadelphia newspaper, but sightings have occurred for centuries. The Devil even influenced the name of a hockey team!

AMERICAN GHOST LEGENDS

Perhaps some of the most fun legends to tell around a campfire are ghost stories. In Texas, one of the most famous ghosts is La Llorona (LAH yoh-ROH-nah). The legend is especially important to the Mexican American community. In Spanish, "La Llorona" means "weeping woman."

There are many **versions** of the legend. One version says that a beautiful young woman had children with a rich man. When he left her, she killed her children. When she died, her soul couldn't rest because of what she had done. Legend has it she wanders around looking for her children. Some even say she tries to steal children away at night.

The Queen Mary

From the 1930s to the 1960s, the huge RMS *Queen Mary* was used as both a passenger ship and warship. Today, *Queen Mary* sits in Long Beach Harbor, California, and is said to be one of the most haunted places in America. Nearly 50 people have died there in the past 60 years, and many visitors report seeing ghosts.

La Llorona is a legend told to children so they know not to go out at night.

11

BLACKBEARD'S GHOST

The fierce pirate Blackbeard terrorized the Atlantic coast in the early 1700s. In 1718, the British navy finally caught up with him and cut off his head. And then legend took over. His headless body reportedly swam around the ship three times before sinking into the ocean!

Today, Blackbeard's ghost is said to haunt the area near North Carolina where he died. Witnesses claim they've seen his body swimming in circles at the spot called Teach's Hole. Many report seeing a strange light glowing beneath the water. Others claim they've seen his ghost rise out of the water and walk ashore carrying a lantern. They believe he's searching for his head.

The Real Blackbeard

The real Blackbeard was probably named Edward Teach. Historians believe he was born in England before 1690. He may have been a sailor during a war between England and Spain. When the war ended, Teach became a pirate. In 1718, Teach blocked the port of Charlestown, South Carolina, with his pirate ships.

Blackbeard

On stormy nights, legend has it you can hear Blackbeard yelling, "Where's my head?"

THE LEGEND OF SLEEPY HOLLOW

In 1820, American author Washington Irving published the short story "The Legend of Sleepy Hollow." It's set in the late 1700s in a Dutch settlement called Sleepy Hollow, near Tarrytown, New York. One night, a schoolteacher named Ichabod Crane was riding home past a graveyard. He knew that a headless soldier was buried there.

Suddenly, a headless man on a horse burst out of the ground. Crane ran and hid, but the horseman found him and threw his head at Ichabod. The next day, the townspeople discovered Ichabod's hat next to a smashed pumpkin, but Ichabod was nowhere to be found. He was never seen again.

Irving's American Legends

Washington Irving also wrote "Rip Van Winkle." In this story, a man named Rip Van Winkle wanders through the Catskill Mountains to avoid his annoying wife. He sees ghosts and drinks a magic potion he got from them, which makes him fall asleep. He doesn't wake up for 20 years!

"The Legend of Sleepy Hollow" became a popular legend, especially in Tarrytown, which people say is still haunted by a headless horseman. It's an important part of local **folklore.**

15

WILD WISCONSIN

Wisconsin is full of monsters! At least that's what the legends say. The Beast of Bray Road is said to live in Elkhorn, Wisconson. The Beast is a werewolf and was first reported in 1949. The creature is said to stand on its hind legs and walk like a human.

Tiny men called Haunches are said to roam Mystic Road in a town named Muskego. The goblinish creatures are said to live in tiny buildings and travel through tunnels beneath their "Haunchyville" to avoid capture by the police. One local man said he was beat up by these creatures one night, but the men were never found.

Wisconsin's Sea Serpents

Devil's Lake in Wisconsin is said to have an octopus-like creature lurking in its waters. Others say it's a prehistoric animal somehow still alive in the lake. At another lake, Lake Mendota, a creature maned Bozho is said to play tricks on beachgoers—tipping canoes and scaring swimmers by tickling their feet.

Werewolves are usually humans that transform into hairy creatures in the light of a full moon. There have been many sightings of werewolves in Wisconsin but the Beast of Bray Road is the most famous.

A MAN LARGER THAN LIFE

There were many odd legends that grew around the western frontier of the United States. Tall tales were spun of legendary men and women who showed their courage and made their mark on the American West.

The story of Paul Bunyan is truly larger than life. It's said that Paul Bunyan was a huge lumberjack, so big that he could shape the land he walked on. Some say it was Paul Bunyan who made the Grand Canyon and great hills and farmland of America. He dug lakes and rivers by hand. He was also a big eater. Legend has it Bunyan ate pancakes so big his grill had to be greased by men wearing bacon skates!

The Strongman's Sidekicks

Every folk hero needs a sidekick, and Paul Bunyan had two! He was said to have a huge ox named Babe. Not only was Babe larger than life—she was blue! Bunyan's bookkeeper Johnny Inkslinger was always by his side recording his accomplishments. Babe and Johnny traveled with Bunyan as he carved out the great American landscape.

19

PECOS BILL AND SLUE-FOOT SUE

Like Paul Bunyan, Pecos Bill grew out of the tall tales of the new frontier. This character was created around the campfires of cowboys, as a **symbol** of strength and bravery.

Legend has it that Pecos Bill was born in the 1830s in Texas. As a baby, he fell out of his parents' wagon and into the Pecos River, where he drifted downstream. He grew up in the wilderness and was raised by wild animals. When he came to live around people, he brought his wildness and strength to his job as a cowboy. Some say he could lasso a whole herd of cattle at once!

Texas state quarter

Slue-Foot Sue

It's said that Pecos Bill fell in love with a woman named Slue-Foot Sue, who was every bit as wild as he was. She even rode a catfish down a river! Pecos Bill wanted to impress Sue, so he shot each star out of the sky except for one. The one he left is the Lone Star, a symbol of Texas.

LEGENDS ON THE RAILS

In the late 1800s, Americans were building railroads all across the country. Mountains posed a challenge, and workers had to carve tunnels straight through them. In West Virginia, the challenge was the Big Bend Tunnel.

One railroad legend says John Henry, a former slave, became a steel driver at this tunnel. Steel drivers hammered a piece of steel into rock to make holes for blasting charges. The first steam drill was invented to make the job easier, but it took jobs away from many workers. Henry bet he could do more work than the machine. Henry won—but he died from **exhaustion** soon after.

The legend may have begun in a folk ballad, or a story set to music. It was especially important to the African American community. The ballad says, "John Henry was a steel drivin' man. He died with a hammer in his hand."

Ghost Trains

Many legends of ghost trains have risen from the railroads. One of the most famous railroad ghost train legends involves Abraham Lincoln's funeral train. In 1865, a train carried Lincoln's body 1,700 miles (2,736 km) from Washington, D.C., to Springfield, Illinois. Afterward, railroad workers reported seeing the ghost of the funeral train riding the rails, with Lincoln's ghost not yet at rest.

23

CREEPY CREATURE LEGENDS

Throughout history, reports of a huge half human, half animal have popped up around the world. In the Himalayan Mountain area of Asia, people believe in a creature called a Yeti. In the American Pacific Northwest, many believe in a similar legend—Bigfoot.

Bigfoot is also called "Sasquatch," which comes from Native American words for "wild man." Native tribes believed in this creature long before settlers reported seeing it. Bigfoot is reportedly up to nine feet (2.7 m) tall, covered in fur, and walks upright. Some believe there are many of these creatures hiding in forests. Bigfoots are said to live in thick forests where they can't be found.

Boggy Creek Monster

People who live in the small town of Fouke, Arkansas, believe a creature lurks around their nearby creeks. Like Bigfoot, the creature is covered in fur and stands more than seven feet (2.1 m) tall. First seen in 1908, the Boggy Creek Monster has been seen by many of the town's citizens and lives on in legend.

So many in the Pacific Northwest are convinced Bigfoot creatures exist that there are laws protecting them. In some counties in Washington, it's illegal to kill a Bigfoot!

SASQUATCH CROSSING

In the southwestern United States, as well as areas of Mexico and Puerto Rico, there are legends of a creature called the chupacabra. The chupacabra is described differently in different areas, but some say it looks like a huge, hairless dog or a bear with fangs. Some even say there are spikes on its back.

Chupacabra means "goat sucker" in Spanish, and many **livestock** deaths are blamed on it. Legend has it the chupacabra leaves livestock drained of blood with fang marks in their neck. Many people report seeing the chupacabra, but others say the creatures are just coyotes with a skin illness called mange.

A Lake Monster Named Champ

Underneath the still waters of Lake Champlain, locals believe there lives a huge monster. Nicknamed Champ, the creature appeared in Native American legends long before European settlers arrived in the area. Legend has it that Champ is a snakelike creature more than 25 feet (7.6 m) long. However, some reports say Champ is more than 75 feet (23 m) long!

The legend of the chupacabra is a young one. The first sightings were in the 1950s. In the 1990s, there was a boom in livestock attacks that were blamed on the chupacabra.

27

KEEPING LEGENDS ALIVE

From the tall tales of the Wild West to legends of creepy creatures, America is rich with exciting and wild stories. Many are a symbol of what's important to Americans—bravery, strength, adventure, and loyalty to one's people. It's also important to keep these legends alive, so they can connect America's future with its past.

Does your town or state have a weird legend? Local legends are stories told in a certain place. They often bring the community together, just as national legends bring the country together. Explore the history around you. You may find some meaningful—and even odd—stories to pass on!

Dover Demon

One cryptid, the Dover Demon, hasn't been spotted in decades. The creature was first spotted by a teenager on April 21, 1977. The next night another teenager claimed to see it, but it hasn't been spotted since. Will you be the next to stumble upon this creature?

Bear Lake Monster

The Bear Lake Monster is an odd legend in the Bear Lake region of Idaho and Utah. This creature was first spotted in 1868. Some say the monster is like a crocodile, but is nearly 40 feet (12 m) long. Others say it's a 90-foot (27 m) snake with legs. Those who live in the region pass on the story, and it's become a part of their local culture.

29

GLOSSARY

cloven hoof: an animal foot that has the front part divided into two

cryptid: an animal or plant that may exist but has not been proven to by science

culture: the beliefs and ways of life of a group of people

exhaustion: the state of being very tired

folklore: ideas or stories that aren't true, but that many people have heard or read

frontier: a part of a country that has been newly opened for settlement

heritage: something handed down from the past

livestock: animals kept or raised for use and profit

methane: a gas known for its foul, rotting eggs–like smell

symbol: a picture or shape that stands for something else

tradition: a long-practiced custom

version: a form of something that is different from others

FOR MORE INFORMATION

BOOKS

Petruccio, Steven James. *American Legends and Tall Tales.* Mineola, NY: Dover Publications, Inc., 2010.

Smith, Andrea P. *Paul Bunyan.* New York, NY: PowerKids Press, 2012.

Worth, Bonnie. *Looking for Bigfoot.* New York, NY: Random House, 2010.

WEBSITES

American Folklore: Myths and Legends
americanfolklore.net/folklore/myths-legends
Learn about more legends that have been told in America for centuries.

The Museum of Unnatural History
unmuseum.org/unmain.htm
Explore the unnatural creatures, landforms, and events in history that have led to some amazing American legends.

31

INDEX